DATE DUE

WHY SHOULD I GO TO BED NOW?

✦ and other questions about a healthy mind ✦

Louise Spilsbury

Heinemann Library
Chicago, Illinois

Designed by David Poole and Tokay Interactive Ltd
Illustrations by Kamae Design Ltd
Originated by Ambassador Litho Ltd
Printed in China by Wing King Tong

07 06 05 04 03
10 9 8 7 6 5 4 3 2 1

Library of Congress Cataloging-in-Publication Data
Spilsbury, Louise.
  Why should I go to bed now? : and other questions about a healthy mind / Louise Spilsbury.
     v. cm. -- (Body matters)
Includes bibliographical references and index.
Contents: Why should I go to bed on time? -- How does my brain work? -- Why should I eat breakfast? -- How can exercise help? -- Why shouldn't I watch TV all day? -- What is stress? -- How can I stop stress? -- Why should I talk about my feelings? -- How can I feel good about myself? -- Amazing facts about the brain.
  ISBN 1-4034-4682-2 (HC)
  1. Brain--Juvenile literature. 2. Brain--Care and hygiene--Juvenile literature. [1. Brain. 2. Mental health. 3. Health.] I. Title. II. Series.
  QP376.S755 2003
  612.8'2--dc21

                                        2003004981

Acknowledgments
The author and publishers are grateful to the following for permission to reproduce copyright material:
pp. 4, 6, 11, 14, 15, 21, 23, 17, 19, 25 Getty Images; pp. 5, 13, 18 Science Photo Library; p. 9 Corbis/Bob Winsett; p. 10 Corbis/Gerhard Steiner; pp. 12, 22 Tudor Phtography; p. 24 Corbis/Huerwitz Creative; p. 26 Corbis/William Gottlieb; p. 27 Corbis/Randy O'Rourke; p. 28 Corbis.

Cover photograph by Tudor Photography.

Every effort has been made to contact copyright holders of any material reproduced in this book. Any omissions will be rectified in subsequent printings if notice is given to the publisher.

Some words are shown in bold, **like this.** You can find out what they mean by looking in the glossary.

CONTENTS

Keep a diary

Throughout the book, there are ideas for keeping a diary. A diary can provide a record of what you eat, the exercises that you do, and what is good for your brain. You can add your own notes to the diary, too.

WHY SHOULD I GO TO BED NOW?

Did you know that you can survive longer without food than you can without sleep? Your body needs the rest it gets while you sleep to recover from the day's activities—and sleep is necessary for a healthy mind.

It is when your mind is busy at night that you dream—but you usually remember a dream only if you wake up during one.

Why does my mind need sleep?

When we talk about your mind, we mean your thoughts, feelings, memories, and moods. Your brain is the part of your body that controls your mind. Unlike most of your body, your brain does not rest while you sleep. It still has to control your heartbeat, breathing, and other body functions. Scientists think that your brain uses your sleeping time to solve problems and sort out the various experiences and new information you learned during the day.

4

What happens when I sleep?

When you fall asleep, your brain tells your body to gradually relax until, after about an hour, you are in a deep sleep. Your body is very still—except for your eyes. At times during your sleep, your eyes move around quickly, as if they are following the thoughts in your mind. This is called REM (rapid eye movement) sleep, and it is when you dream.

HOW MUCH SLEEP DO I NEED?

You need different amounts of sleep at different stages in your life. Babies sleep for about sixteen hours a day. Teenagers need about eight hours, while older people may need only six hours. Young people need up to ten hours of sleep, but you may find that you need more or less.

Using special equipment, scientists can tell when a person's mind is active during sleep. When the brain is busy, wiggly lines show up on the chart.

TIPS FOR A GOOD NIGHT'S SLEEP

If you have trouble falling asleep at night, try these tips.

- Try to go to bed at roughly the same time each day to get your body into a routine.

- Take a warm bath to relax before bedtime.

- Have a warm milky drink and avoid drinking tea, coffee, or soda late in the day because these can keep you awake.

- Try reading a book or listening to some music before going to bed.

Missing out on sleep can mean missing out on a lot of fun or learning the following day. Sleep is vital for keeping your body and mind healthy and happy.

What happens if I do not get enough sleep?

When you do not get enough sleep, you feel tired and grumpy, and you may act a little clumsily. You may have trouble concentrating on your schoolwork or find that you argue more with your friends.

HOW DOES MY BRAIN WORK?

Your brain is like a living computer, but one that is far more powerful and clever than any machine. Every moment of the day, whether you are asleep or awake, your brain is dealing with a huge range of complicated tasks.

The brain is the control center of your body. It looks a little like a big, gray, wrinkly walnut. The brain is made up of different parts, each with a different job to do. **Nerves** are like your body's private telephone system. Messages travel to your brain from the rest of your body—and back again—along nerves that pass through your spinal cord (inside your backbone).

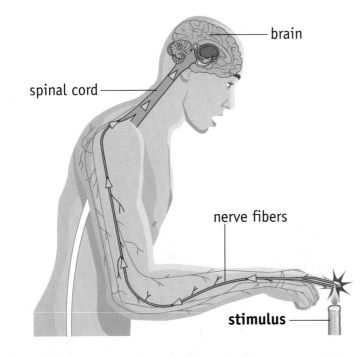

brain

spinal cord

nerve fibers

stimulus

Information about the world around you passes from your senses along nerve fibers in your spinal cord to your brain. Your brain stores this information so you can learn from your experiences.

The parts of a brain

The cerebrum is the largest part of the brain. It does most of your thinking, based on information from your senses, and tells the rest of your body what to do. It has two halves. The right half controls the left side of your body and the left half controls the right side of your body.

The hypothalamus sits beneath the thalamus. It controls your body temperature and deals with sensations such as hunger or tiredness.

The thalamus sorts nerve signals that come through the brain stem. It sends them to the different parts of the brain.

The cerebellum controls your automatic body movements, such as balancing your body when you ride a bike.

The hippocampus is a tiny but important part of the cerebrum. It deals with memories of things that happened recently and long ago.

The brain stem connects the rest of the brain to the spinal cord. It controls basic body functions, such as breathing, **circulation**, and **digestion**.

8

How does my mind work?

The outer layer of the brain's cerebrum is called the cerebral cortex. Scientists believe this is the part of your brain that is responsible for your thoughts and feelings. Your cerebral cortex does the work when you write an essay, draw a picture, or imagine your future.

To have a healthy mind, you need to take care of the body part that controls it—your brain. The bones of your skull form a protective box around your brain, but you should still wear a helmet when you ride a bike or skateboard.

MIND-BOGGLING

People use many different phrases about the mind. If you have a "clear head" or can "think straight," it means that your mind is ready for the task ahead. When you need to "clear your mind," you may be confused and need some time to focus.

WHY SHOULD I EAT BREAKFAST?

No one expects a battery-operated toy to work without batteries or a car to start without gasoline. Your brain is a kind of natural machine. Like the rest of your body, it needs fuel to give it **energy** to work properly. Your body fuel is food, and after a long night without eating, your body urgently needs to recharge!

Breakfast boost

Think of the many ways you use your brain every morning at school—it helps you talk, read, do math problems, answer questions, and write. Tests have shown that students who skip breakfast cannot concentrate as well as those who have had a good breakfast.

A fast is when you go without food for a long time. By morning, it can be about fourteen hours since you last ate. You "break your fast" to recharge your brain and body.

How does breakfast help?

When you eat, your body turns food into energy by a process called **digestion.** This is when food is broken down in your stomach and intestines. Most of the food you eat is broken down into **glucose,** a kind of sugar. The glucose passes into your blood and is carried to all parts of your body, including your brain. Your body uses glucose to make the energy it needs.

Some body parts, such as **muscles,** can store glucose for later, but your brain needs a constant supply. After a night without food, your brain's glucose levels are very low, and it needs a new supply to get going again.

Your brain is the greediest part of your body. When it is working hard, it uses up more energy than even your heart, which has to pump blood all around your body 24 hours a day.

What makes a healthy breakfast?

Like any other meal, breakfast should include a mix of the five **nutrients** to be healthy. **Carbohydrates**—found in cereals, bread, bagels, muffins, and grains—are very important. The body converts carbohydrates into **glucose** to give you **energy** all morning. Dairy products such as milk, eggs, and cheese, along with nuts and peanut butter, give you some **protein, minerals,** and **fat.** A glass of fruit juice or a piece of fruit gives you a dose of **vitamins.**

If you are too busy to eat breakfast, make a change. Get up fifteen minutes earlier, or pack a breakfast and eat it on your way!

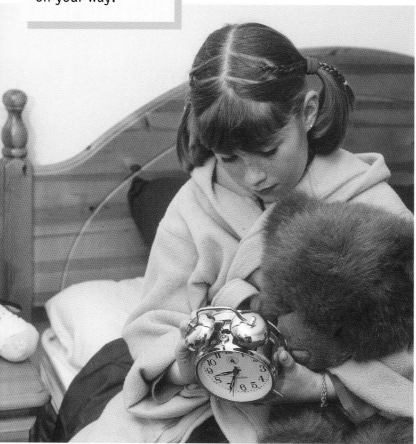

The important thing about a healthy breakfast is to have a mix of nutrients—it does not matter what you eat. If cold pizza, a tuna sandwich, or even a bowl of soup gets you started, then go for it!

Keep a diary

Keep a record of what you eat for breakfast for two weeks. Then look back and figure out if you were feeding your brain a good variety of nutrients. Score each breakfast on a scale of one to ten, ten being the healthiest. What can you do to raise your breakfast score?

This special picture of a brain shows the large area of fluid inside it (the yellow and red parts). As your brain uses this liquid, you need to replace it by drinking plenty of water.

Water on the brain

Do not forget to drink lots of water, too. You might not be able to hear it sloshing around when you move your head, but your brain contains lots of liquid, called cerebrospinal fluid. It is made up almost entirely of water. You need to drink at least six glasses of water a day to keep your brain—and the rest of your body—healthy.

13

HOW CAN EXERCISE HELP?

Have you ever gone for a walk to clear your head? It is a fact that your head—your mind—often feels clearer and more alert after exercise. Scientists are still not sure why this is, but most believe that it is because exercise increases the amount of **glucose** and **oxygen** that gets to your brain. This gives your brain more **energy.**

Why does walking clear my head?

When you exercise you breathe faster to take in more oxygen from the air.

When you walk, your leg **muscles** need extra energy, which they make by using glucose from your food and oxygen from the air. Your body collects more oxygen from the air by breathing faster. Your heart beats faster to pump the blood, which carries the glucose and oxygen through your **circulation** system—the blood vessels all over your body.

As blood passes through your brain, it brings the extra oxygen and glucose there, too. Your brain uses these to produce energy. As blood passes through the different parts of the body, it also collects waste left over from energy production. Blood traveling through the brain removes waste, so your brain really should feel clearer after exercise!

Exercise for relaxation

Exercise also helps your brain because it helps you to relax. This might seem like a contradiction, because we have just seen how exercise makes your mind more alert. Although your brain feels more active right after exercising, later you feel relaxed. Your body is tired out, so you sleep more soundly—and getting a good night's sleep is important for a healthy mind.

Do not exercise right before bedtime because this can keep you awake. Allow your body a couple of hours to wind down after you have been active.

Keep a diary

Keep a record in your diary of the exercise you do each day for two weeks. Write down your mood and how clear your mind felt before and after you exercised. When you look back over your entries, do you find that exercise was good for your brain?

Think positive!

Exercise also helps you to think and feel more positive about things. This is because your body releases chemicals called endorphins when you are active. These produce a feeling of well-being or happiness in your brain. When you feel happier and more positive, you can deal better with people, schoolwork, and the rest of your life.

Exercise can change your mood! It can take your mind off your troubles, and it increases the amount of chemicals that create positive feelings in the brain.

Which exercise is best?

It does not really matter what sort of exercise you do—just choose activities that you enjoy and try to do several different things each week. These can include walking to school or to a friend's house, taking a dance class, swimming, biking, and going to gym class. It is not hard to find ways to get enough exercise. Try to do about 20 minutes everyday.

Exercise—alone or on a team—makes your mind and body healthier.

Team sports

There are times when team sports can have a negative effect on your mind. This happens when games become too competitive and people feel unhappy if their team loses or if they let the team down. Most of the time, though, playing on a team makes people feel more positive. Along with exercise, it gives people a chance to share experiences. It is a good way to make new friends.

WHY SHOULDN'T I WATCH TV ALL DAY?

Like any other part of your body, your brain needs exercise to keep it healthy. Watching TV is okay sometimes, but your brain needs a mix of activities to be in top form.

Making connections

This picture shows brain neurons. The blobs are the main parts of the nerve cells, and the lines are fibers that carry electrical signals.

Your brain is made up of millions of **nerve cells,** called neurons, which look like tiny bundles of fibers. When you are born, you have all your neurons, but most are not connected to each other. When you learn or do something new, **electrical signals** carry information between the neurons. This connects them, making pathways for more signals to pass along. This is why it may seem hard when you try something new, such as swimming, but it seems easy once you have learned to do it—because the neuron connections have all been made.

What are the best brain boosters?

Different areas of your brain are responsible for different activities. Because of this, if you do only one thing, you will exercise only one part of your brain. It is important to do lots of different activities. In addition to activities that you might expect to exercise your brain— such as reading and drawing— simply experiencing new sights, sounds, and smells will also exercise it.

BRAIN BOOSTERS

Doing things differently creates new pathways between neurons and exercises neurons that are not used much. Try these brain boosters:

- Take a new route to a friend's house.

- Brush your teeth with the hand that you do not normally use.

- Learn some card tricks or try juggling.

- Eat some spicy foods that you have not tried before.

Try solving crosswords or other brainteasers to get your brain working.

WHAT IS STRESS?

Have you ever found it hard to get to sleep because of a test the next day? Have you ever felt upset or sick because you were worried about an argument you had with a friend? This is what it is like to feel stress. It is not only adults who can feel stressed—young people can, too.

How does stress feel?

You feel stress when you are worried, afraid, or angry about something for a long time. These thoughts and feelings build up in your mind until they make your body feel ill. Some people say that stress gives them a headache or stomachache, or makes it hard to relax and go to sleep.

Sometimes when people are stressed, they cannot think of anything else and find it hard to concentrate.

Can some stress be good?

In certain situations, a little stress can be helpful—for example, before you perform in a school play. When you feel nervous, your body makes a chemical called adrenaline. It speeds up your heartbeat and your breathing so that you can make **energy** faster. This makes you more alert and ready for action.

The problem is that other parts of your body slow down to provide you with the extra energy you need to deal with stress. You do not eat or sleep as well, and your body becomes weaker. This means that you are more likely to catch **infections** that make you ill.

Do you feel butterflies in your stomach when you are worried about something? It happens because blood is rushing to your brain, where you are using a lot of energy, and away from your stomach, leaving it feeling strange and fluttery.

HOW CAN I STOP STRESS?

If you feel stressed because you have a lot of homework and activities, make a schedule. Check it every day to make sure you do all you need to do, but remember to give yourself enough time to rest and relax, too!

The first step in dealing with stress is deciding what is causing it. Then you can figure out how to cope with it. Stress is often caused by things you can change—for example, if you are having trouble with homework or a subject at school.

If you are worried about a test or a performance, one of the best remedies is practice. If you are well prepared, you will feel better. If you are stuck on schoolwork, ask for help. If you keep forgetting to do your homework, write a note or make a schedule to remind you to get the work done when you need to.

What else can help?

Some of the things you should be doing to keep your whole body well—eating healthy food, getting enough sleep, and exercising—will also help you stop stress. Many people find that taking up a new hobby can also help. Your new hobby could be something restful, such as knitting or drawing, or a new challenge, such as learning a new instrument or joining a band.

Do not overdo it, though. Having too much to do in a week can become a cause of stress itself. Make sure you have some time to relax as well, perhaps by reading a book or just soaking in the tub.

When you feel stressed, try this breathing exercise to help you relax. Breathe in deeply and slowly through your nose. Then breathe out slowly through your mouth. Do this about four times.

WHY SHOULD I TALK ABOUT MY FEELINGS?

As you near **puberty**—the years when you begin to change from a child into an adult—it is perfectly natural to have more mood changes. Sometimes you may feel angry or upset without really knowing why. If you discuss a problem with someone, it often makes you feel better.

Some people find that writing or drawing about their feelings is a helpful way of working through them.

How does talking help?

When you talk to someone about a problem, the other person may be able to help you solve it. Talking about your feelings also makes you feel better because it releases some of the stress that can make you feel ill. Sometimes you need to find other ways of dealing with your feelings. If you can feel yourself losing your temper, try counting to ten or walking away from the situation.

Who should I talk to?

It can help to talk to friends—you may find it a comfort to know that they feel just like you do sometimes. When something is really bothering you, though, it is better to talk to a parent or to another adult because they have more experience. They also care about you very much—even if they get angry with you sometimes.

Pick a time to talk with someone when neither of you are busy, and make sure that you do not get interrupted.

If you do not want to talk to someone in your family, talk to a teacher or to someone else you trust, such as a school nurse. If you prefer, you could call a free helpline, which you can find in most telephone directories. These are open day and night, and the people who answer them give advice about all kinds of problems.

What can I do about bullying?

Many people feel unhappy or stressed because of bullying at some point in their lives. Bullies are people who hurt others by calling them names or by hitting them or pushing them around.

It can be difficult to know what to do about bullying. Some people find that if they ignore the bully, he or she gets bored and leaves them alone. This is not always the case, though. You may need to talk to an adult you can trust, such as a parent or a teacher. The adult should be able to get someone to talk to the bully and stop his or her bad behavior. This is not tattling—bullying is wrong, and it is right and important that it is stopped.

If you see someone being teased or bullied, talk to a teacher about it when no one else is around.

HOW CAN I FEEL GOOD ABOUT MYSELF?

Feeling good about yourself and proud of who you are is called self-esteem. Self-esteem is very important to keep you both happy and healthy.

How do I get self-esteem?

Self-esteem is not something you are born with or something you can buy. People learn self-esteem from parents, caregivers, or teachers. You can also improve your own self-esteem.

- Pat yourself on the back when you do something right and do not dwell on things you do wrong. If you fail a test, think about what you do well.

- Be realistic. Nobody is perfect, and we need to accept the things we cannot change.

- Play for fun, not just to win.

- Take up a new hobby—-you may be really good at it.

Self-esteem gives you the courage to make new friends and try new challenges.

What if I make mistakes?

To have a healthy mind, you need to look after your body, live a full life, and find ways of dealing with difficult times.

If you do something wrong, it does not mean that you are a bad person. We live in a world where ads and TV programs show perfect people living perfect lives. When real life turns out to be different, it can be easy to think that something is wrong. In real life, though, everyone makes mistakes, and mistakes are an important part of how we develop. You should never feel like a failure because of mistakes you make. Just make sure that you learn from them.

When you have good self-esteem, you are less likely to make serious mistakes. When you respect and trust your own judgment, you will have the confidence to say no if someone suggests doing something that you know is wrong.

AMAZING FACTS ABOUT THE BRAIN

- When you are born, your brain is about one-quarter of its adult size.

- You have about 100 billion **nerve cells,** or neurons, in your brain. That is about as many stars as there are in a galaxy!

- Messages traveling from your body parts to your brain through your spinal cord travel at more than 180 miles (300 kilometers) per hour—as fast as the fastest trains.

- The world's heaviest-known human brain weighed 5 pounds (2.3 kilograms). It belonged to a man who was 30 years old.

- The skull that protects your brain is not a single bone. Rather, it is made up of 28 different bones that all fit together perfectly.

- Although your brain can tell you about things that your skin feels, it cannot feel things itself. Doctors can operate on a brain while the patient is awake without the patient feeling any pain.

GLOSSARY

carbohydrate   nutrient in food that gives you energy

circulation   process by which blood vessels (tubes) carry blood around your body

digestion   way the body breaks down food

electrical signals   way that information passes invisibly through nerves or wires

energy   power that allows living things to do everything they need to live and grow

fat   nutrient found in foods such as butter and oil

glucose   sugar that your body uses to make energy

infection   kind of disease that can be spread to other people

mineral   chemical found in rocks and soil. Similar substances found in foods are nutrients needed for your body to be healthy.

muscles   bunches of fibers that move the different parts of your body

nerve cells   building blocks of nerves in the body

nerves   pathways that carry messages to and from the brain

nutrients   chemicals in food that are good for you

oxygen   gas in the air that we need to breathe

protein nutrient in some foods that your body can use to build or repair body parts

puberty stage in life when your body begins to develop from a child into an adult

stimulus something that triggers a response, often from your senses

vitamin nutrient found in certain foods that your body needs to be healthy

FURTHER READING

Ayer, Eleanor H. *Everything You Need to Know about Stress.* New York: Rosen, 2001.

Gregson, Susan R. *Stress Management.* Mankato, Minn.: Capstone, 2000.

Silverstein, Alvin, and Virginia B. Silverstein. *Sleep.* Danbury, Conn.: Scholastic Library, 2000.

INDEX